ALLSORTS

BY THE SEASHORE

by Jenny Vaughan

Macdonald

Factual Adviser: Dr A L Rice,
Institute of Oceanographic Sciences
Deacon Laboratory

Editor: Heather Ancient
Teacher Panel: Tim Firth,
Ann Merriman, Helen Walklett
Designer: Sally Boothroyd
Production: Rosemary Bishop

Illustrations
Nichola Armstrong: 20–21, 22–23, 26–27
Peter Bull: 28–29
Anna Hancock: 8–9, 16–17, 18–19
Kevin Maddison: 10–11, 12–13, 24–25
Sheila Ratcliffe: 6–7, 14–15

'Lightships' from *Collected Poems* by
Clive Sansom, is reprinted by permission
of Methuen and David Higham Associates Ltd

A MACDONALD BOOK

© Macdonald & Co (Publishers) Ltd 1989

First published in Great Britain in 1989 by
Macdonald & Co (Publishers) Ltd
London & Sydney
A member of Maxwell Pergamon Publishing
Corporation plc

Printed and bound in Great Britain by
Purnell Book Production Ltd
A member of BPCC plc

Macdonald & Co (Publishers) Ltd
66-73 Shoe Lane
London EC4P 4AB

British Library Cataloguing in Publication Data
Vaughan, Jennifer, *1947–*
   By the seashore. – (Allsorts; 5)
   1. Seashore. Organisms – For children
   2. Seaside resorts. Social life, to 1988
   I. Title II. Series
   574.909′46
   ISBN 0–356–13451–2
   ISBN 0–356–13965–4 Pbk

How to use this book

First look at the contents page
opposite, to see if the subject you
want is there. For instance, if you
want to find out about rocky
shores, you will find the
information on pages 18 and 19.
At the end of the book you will
find a word list. This explains
some of the more difficult words
found in this book. There is also
an index. Use it if you want to
find out about one particular
thing. For instance, if you want
to find out about sharks, the
index tells you there is something
about them on page 23.

CONTENTS

BRIGHT AND EARLY

Many people like to go to the seaside in summer to swim and sunbathe. On a hot day the beach can become very crowded and noisy.

The beach is much quieter in the early morning. Most people are still in bed. But the birds and animals that live along the seashore are up and about searching for food.

The quietest beaches are the ones that people hardly ever visit. These beaches can be hard to get to and there are no hotels, shops or restaurants there. Many different kinds of birds and animals can live there in peace.

redshank

oyster catcher

avocet

ringed plover

These birds are all kinds of waders. They wade in shallow water when the tide is out.

They poke their bills into the mud and sand. They are looking for worms and other small animals to eat.

Twice a day, the sea comes high up the beach. This is high tide. At high tide the sea covers most of the beach. Then each wave breaks further down the beach until it is low tide and you can explore more of the beach.

On some beaches, cleaners are at work early in the morning. They clear away the rubbish that has been left behind by careless people. They also clear away the seaweed and dead sea animals that the tide washes up.

Sometimes fishing boats work through the night. In the morning they unload the catch in the harbour.

In some places, if you go to the harbour early in the morning, you can buy fresh fish for breakfast.

SUNSHINE AND SAND

Do you go to the seaside for your holidays? Many people do. But things were not always like that. Two hundred years ago, few people had holidays at all. No one thought of going to the seaside for a holiday. Hardly anyone could swim and it was not fashionable to sunbathe.

Then doctors began to think that sea bathing and breathing sea air could make sick people well. So people started going to the seaside to get better. More and more people found they enjoyed the seaside. Some went by train, just for the day. Others stayed for a longer holiday.

These days many people like to go to other countries for their holidays. They often choose warm, sunny places like Greece or Spain.

People got changed in bathing machines. Then a horse pulled the machine into the sea and the bather stepped straight into the water.

People used to swim with nothing on. But when the seaside became more popular, swimming costumes were invented. The first costumes were very different to the ones we wear today.

1885

1901

1988

One, two, three,
   four, five,
Once I caught
   a fish alive.
Six, seven, eight,
   nine, ten,
Then I let him
   go again.
Why did you let
   him go?
Because he bit
   my finger so.
Which finger did
   he bite?
This little finger
   on the right!

These children are watching a Punch and Judy show. It is a very old kind of puppet show. The show is about a wicked man called Punch, his wife, Judy, and their baby. There is a greedy crocodile in the story who steals Punch's sausages.

Make a Punch and Judy crocodile puppet from an old sock. Cut eyes and nostrils from felt or paper. Cut jagged teeth from paper. Cut the mouth from felt. Glue on the eyes, teeth and mouth. Stuff the toe of the sock with tissues to make it firm. Put your hand inside. Can your crocodile bite?

BESIDE THE SEASIDE

There are lots of things to do at the seaside.
You can play games on the beach and in the
water. You can go sailing or windsurfing. On
some beaches there are donkeys to ride or little
boats you can pedal on the sea.

There are things to do away from the beach,
too. Adults may like to go to a disco in the
evenings. There may be a theatre with a show
for people to see. In many seaside towns there is
a pier stretching out to sea. There may be an
amusement arcade on the pier, with slot
machines and a bingo hall.

Surfing is fun, but it can be
dangerous. So can other
water sports. Lifeguards
help keep people safe.

They put up flags to warn
when the sea is too rough
for swimming. They save
people from drowning.

In Australia there are
many sandy beaches with
big, strong waves where
people can enjoy surfing.
If you go surfing in cold
water you need a wet suit
to keep you warm.

The sand yacht is pushed along the beach by the wind. If the wind is blowing hard the sand yacht can travel very fast.

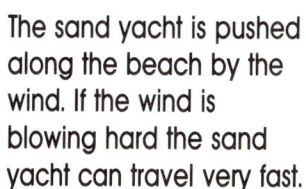

You can see dolphins at a dolphinarium. They are taught to perform tricks to entertain the crowd.

Their tricks are fun to watch. But many people believe it is cruel to keep them away from the open sea.

Some seaside towns have a funfair with exciting rides. Here you can ride on the roundabout or go high into the sky on the big wheel.

An empty beach is a good place for sport. These children live on an island in the Caribbean. There is lots of room to play cricket on the beaches here.

WORKING BY THE SEA

Many people work by the seashore. Some of them work in shops and hotels. Some work on the beach looking after deckchairs or donkey rides. Summer is always their busiest time.

Some of the people who work by the sea are busy all year round. Naturalists study the wild animals of the seashore. They find out if the animals are being harmed by the chemicals and rubbish that are dumped in the sea.

There are people who care for sick and injured sea animals. If an oil tanker is damaged or wrecked, the oil may pour into the sea. Birds and seals can get covered with it. They must be cleaned and looked after or they will die.

When the sun is shining on a summer day it's nice to eat outside beside the sea. Summer is a busy time for the people who work in cafés by the sea.

Long ago, smugglers brought things like brandy and tobacco into this country. They did not want to pay the taxes on these. They landed their boats on lonely beaches where no one would see them. Today, customs officers check that people are not trying to smuggle things in their luggage.

New boats are built in a boatyard. Boats are repaired and cleaned here, too. Seaweed and shellfish attach themselves to the bottoms of boats and must be scraped off.

The coastguards make sure people are safe at sea. They can contact ships by radio to let them know the safest route.

When people need help, the coastguards alert the lifeboats. Sometimes they send a helicopter, or ask other ships to help out.

Coastguards also rescue climbers stuck on cliffs. They may climb the cliff to reach the person. If the climber is injured or hard to reach they may need to send for a helicopter.

SAND BETWEEN OUR TOES

Not all beaches are sandy. Some are covered with pebbles. Some are rocky. Some have thick, sticky mud. Which sort do you like best?

Sand starts off as rock. The waves break the rock up into stones. The tide and the waves make these stones roll backwards and forwards on the sea bed. As they roll, they wear away and become smaller and smaller. After many, many years they are tiny grains of sand.

Some hotel owners like a sandy beach nearby so people will want to stay there. If the beach isn't sandy they can have sand put there. But the tides may slowly wash the sand away again.

Coconut palms often grow near sandy beaches in hot countries. When coconuts fall on to the beach, the tide can carry them away across the sea. If they are washed up on another shore they may grow into new trees.

Big mounds of sand by the sea are called dunes. The wind blows the sand into dunes and can blow the dunes over the land.

To stop this happening people plant grass and other plants on the dunes. Their roots hold the sand and stop it blowing away.

Sand can be different colours. It may be yellow or brown. If there is a volcano nearby it may be black. In hot countries sand is often white because it is made from the skeletons of dead corals.

It's fun to make a picture using sand. Paint a picture with glue on dark paper. Sprinkle sand over the glue. Perhaps you can find sand in more than one colour. Sprinkle different colours on different parts of the picture. Shake off the loose sand when the glue is dry.

Sandbanks are mounds of sand under the sea. They are especially dangerous at low tide. Boats can get stuck on them and may be wrecked. Buoys are used to mark sandbanks.

LIFE ON THE BEACH

A sandy beach may look quite empty. But it isn't. There are hundreds of worms living in the sand. You can see their casts lying on top of wet sand. Some shellfish live in the sand too. You can find their empty shells lying along the beach.

All kinds of things are washed up by the tide. You may find dead sea animals and seaweed. Tiny insects and other animals will eat the dead plants and animals. They cannot eat all the rubbish people leave behind, so you should always take your rubbish home with you.

You may find this interesting thing washed up on the beach. It is called a mermaid's purse. It is the egg case laid by a dogfish. The young dogfish has hatched out and left the case behind.

Jellyfish float in the sea. Sometimes they are left stranded on the shore by the tide. They cannot live out of water. Some can sting you very badly.

You might find the shell of a sea urchin on the beach. Living sea urchins are covered with spines. These get broken off when the sea urchin is dead.

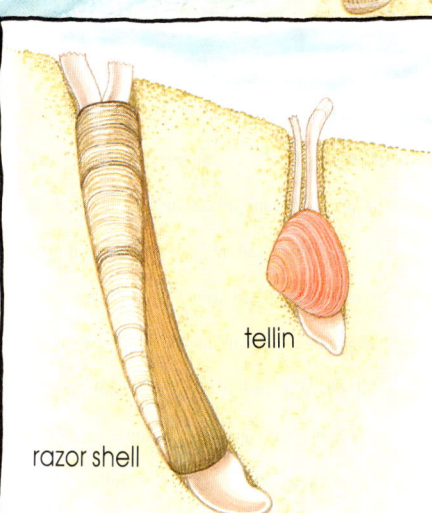

razor shell

tellin

Millions of tiny plants and animals live in the sea. Shellfish in the sand suck in sea water and eat the tiny plants and animals. There is food in the sand too. The lugworm eats wet sand, uses up the food in it and passes the sand out.

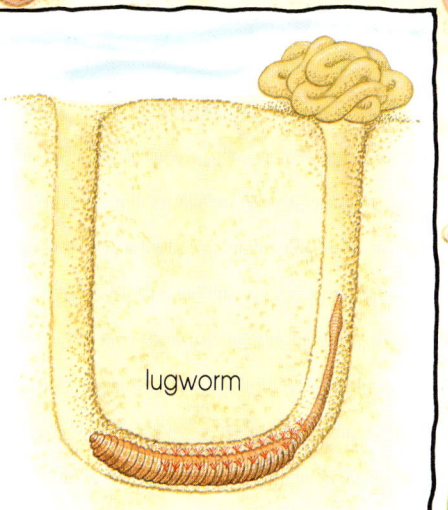

lugworm

The cuttlefish is a relation of the octopus. It has a shell inside its body. You can sometimes see its shell washed up on the beach. They are sold in pet shops for cage birds to peck.

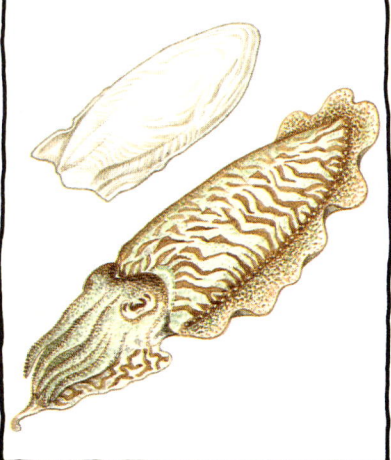

Seals live in wild, lonely places. They live in the sea most of the time, but have their pups on land. Grey seal pups stay ashore until they are three weeks old.

In stormy weather, young seals are sometimes washed up on the shore. They need rest and sleep so if you are lucky enough to see one, don't disturb it.

ROCKY SHORES

Rocky seashores make a good home for many plants and animals. You will see different kinds of seaweed clinging to the rocks. Some kinds are covered by the sea all the time. Others grow on rocks that are out of water at low tide. See how many different kinds you can find.

When the tide goes out you can find little pools left behind among the rocks. These are good places to look for seashore animals. The pools are home for animals such as crabs, shrimps and sea anemones. You may see a starfish or a sea urchin. There may even be a small octopus hiding among the rocks.

You can find mussels and barnacles clinging to the rocks. When the tide is in, they take in tiny pieces of food floating in the sea. Limpets cling to rocks too. They eat the tiny plants which grow on the rocks.

Some people believe you can use seaweed to find out if it will rain. Hang some outside for a few days. People say that it will rain if the seaweed is damp. Is this true? Seaweed can be used in other ways too. Some kinds can be eaten.

The hermit crab does not have its own shell. Instead it lives in an empty sea snail's shell.

If a starfish loses an arm it can grow a new one. Sometimes the broken off arm can grow a new body.

You might see these animals in a rock pool. The anemones look like flowers, but they are really animals. They have arms called tentacles. They eat small animals which they catch in their tentacles. When the tide goes out the anemones pull in their tentacles so they do not dry out. Then they look like lumps of jelly on the rocks.

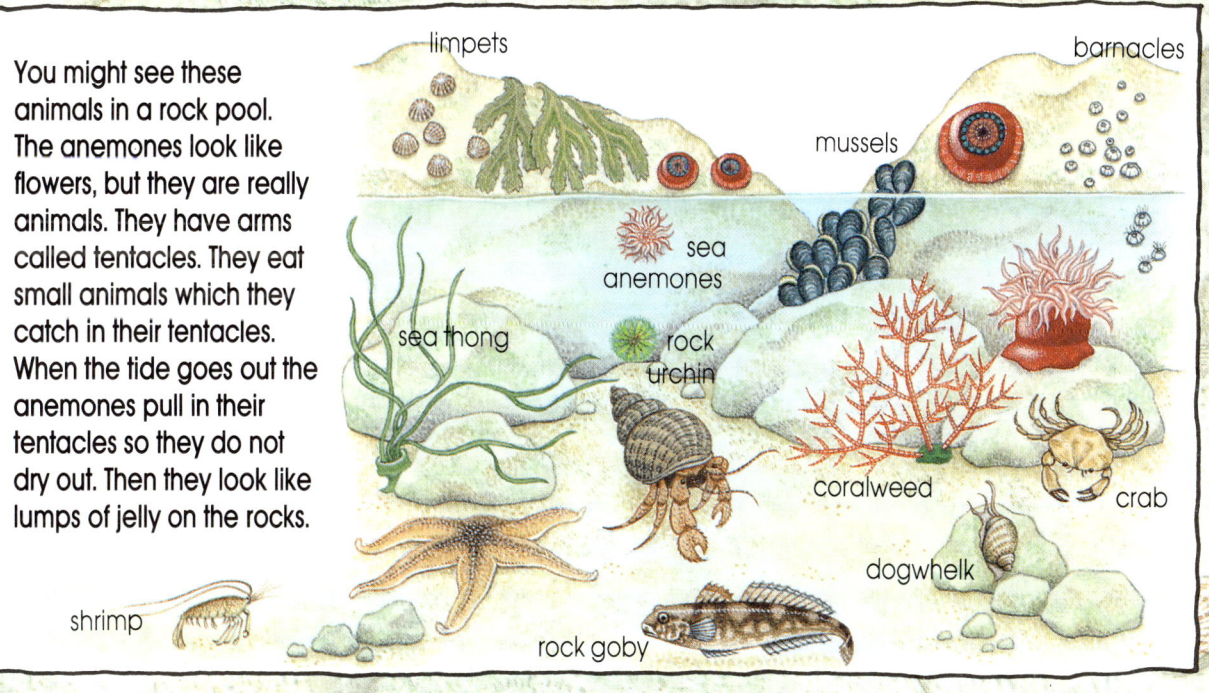

limpets

barnacles

mussels

sea anemones

sea thong

rock urchin

coralweed

crab

dogwhelk

shrimp

rock goby

UP ON THE CLIFF TOP

Some seaside places have cliffs along the shore. Be careful not to go too close to the edge of the cliff. The edges often crumble away and you might fall. Cliffs are often rocky and the beach is a long way down.

At first sight you may think there is nothing interesting on the cliffside. But plants and animals can live on these steep cliffs. Many sea birds make their nests on the cliffs where other animals cannot harm their eggs.

The sea beats against the cliffs and slowly wears the rocks away. Sometimes the rocks are worn into interesting shapes. The sea can also wear holes in the rocks to make caves.

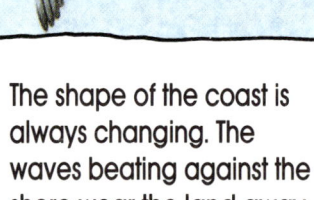

Lighthouses are sometimes built on high cliffs. A lighthouse has a bright light. This flashes at night and warns ships that they are near a rocky shore.

The shape of the coast is always changing. The waves beating against the shore wear the land away.

Houses and villages built on the cliff can fall into the sea when the land under them is eaten away.

Puffins make their nests in holes near the cliff-top. Their beaks are brightly coloured. They eat fish. A puffin can hold about 30 small fish in its beak!

Guillemots are good fliers and fast swimmers. They live in large groups on rocky cliffs. Their eggs are a special shape so that they won't roll off the cliff.

ichthyosaur

ammonite

fossil cockle

Cliffs are good places to find fossils. Fossils are the remains of animals and plants that lived millions of years ago. Mary Anning lived in the 1800s. When she was 11 she found the fossil of an ichthyosaur. It was a sea animal that lived nearly 300 million years ago.

CORAL REEFS

Corals are tiny animals that live in the sea. Each one has a hard skeleton. Some corals are brightly coloured. Living corals often look more like plants or flowers than animals.

Corals live in groups. They grow faster when they live in warm water. After a while the group of corals grows quite large and makes a hard bank called a reef. Sometimes the reef makes a wall or barrier between the shore and the open sea. This is called a barrier reef.

You can see coral reefs in many warm parts of the world. The biggest coral reef is the Great Barrier Reef off the east coast of Australia.

The stonefish lives on coral reefs. It has twelve spines on its back. These spines have poison in them. People on the reef must take care. If they tread on the stonefish they can be stung and poisoned.

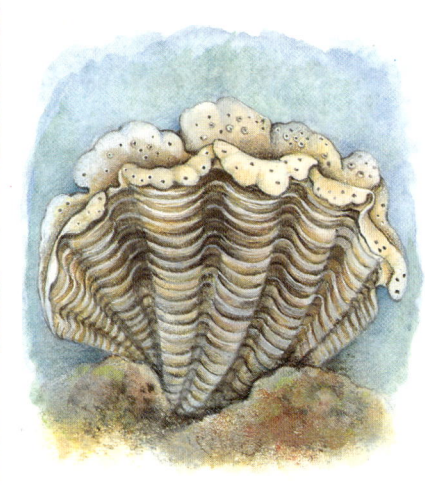

The biggest shellfish of all lives in warm seas. It is the giant clam. It can be a metre across.

You may like to buy pretty shells. But some people kill shellfish so they can sell their shells. If this happens too often, the animals will die out.

angel fish

sea cucumber

sea slug

Sharks are large fish. They are hunters. A hungry shark may attack people in the water. A barrier reef can stop it coming close to the shore.

Corals are very beautiful. People travel from all over the world to see the corals on the Great Barrier Reef.

You can dive down to see the coral. Or you can see it from a boat which has a glass panel in the bottom.

starfish

Hundreds of animals live on the reef. You can see brightly coloured fish, starfish and sea slugs. Sea cucumbers look a bit like ordinary cucumbers, but they are really animals.

STORMY SEAS

The seaside isn't always a sunny place where people can sunbathe and swim. Sometimes there are storms. When the wind blows hard it makes huge waves. They crash on to the beach. These large waves can damage walls, roads and buildings built along the shore.

In a bad storm, the sea is too rough for the boats to go out. They must shelter in the harbour. Even the gulls cannot go out to sea and catch fish. They have to stay inland and look for food there.

Storms can happen at any time of year and in any part of the world. Winter storms are cold as well as rough. In some places it gets so cold in winter that the sea freezes.

Lifeboats go out in stormy weather and rescue people from shipwrecks. The members of a lifeboat's crew are often fishermen.

In some parts of the Soviet Union the sea freezes in winter. The ice is not solid though, there is sea water underneath. People who want to go fishing make holes in the ice to reach the fish in the sea below.

Penguins live in the Antarctic. Their fat bodies and waterproof feathers keep them warm.

Polar bears live in the Arctic. They have thick fur coats to keep out the cold.

When waves break, they become white foam and spray. When this happens out at sea it looks like horses galloping to the shore. So these waves are called 'white horses'.

Many sea birds fly south for the winter. Barnacle geese spend the summer in the Arctic. They nest there and have their young. When the cold Arctic winter comes, they fly south to warmer places like Scotland.

Very strong winds are called hurricanes or typhoons. They mainly blow in the warmer parts of the world. These high winds can do a lot of damage to anything in their path.

NIGHT AT THE SEASIDE

At night, the seashore seems quiet. The gulls and other sea birds are asleep. Many of the fish are asleep, too. Seals sleep under the water. They keep coming to the surface to breathe. They do this while they are still asleep.

But some seashore animals come out at night when it is cool and there is no sun to dry them out. Small animals often come out when the animals that like to eat them are asleep.

Some people are busy, too. In some places the fishing boats go out at night. On stormy nights, the lifeboats may be called out to rescue people.

Try looking for crabs on the beach when the tide is out. They like to come out at night when it is cooler and safer for them.

Loggerhead turtles live in warm seas. The females lay their eggs on the beach at night. They dig a hole in the sand and bury their eggs in it. Loud noises will frighten them away so it is important not to disturb them.

At night-time seagulls look for a place to sleep. If you live by the sea you may have seagulls roosting on your roof every night.

If you are out in a boat on a dark night, you might see flashes of light when waves break. This is sometimes called 'sea fire'.

It is caused by millions of very tiny sea creatures. Their bodies contain chemicals which make them shine in the dark.

Lightships

All night long when the wind is high
Nnn nnn nnnn
The lightships moan and moan to the sky
Nnn nnn nnnn

The foghorns whine when the mist runs free
Nnn nnn nnnn
Warning the men on the ships at sea
Nnn nnn nnnn

Clive Sansom

THINGS TO DO

BIRD MASKS

You can make yourself look like an oystercatcher by making a mask.

Fold a piece of stiff paper in half. The picture shows you the shape to draw. Cut it out. Make an eye hole through both pieces of paper. Cut a little hole in the fold for your nose. Colour the mask.

Draw the shape of the beak on another piece of folded paper. Make the edge that joins it to the mask straight. Cut the beak out. Stick the edges of the two pieces of beak together with sticky tape. Leave the straight edges open. Colour the beak. Fold the straight edges over. Make little cuts in the folded edges so you can open the beak out. Stick the edges to the mask with tape.

Tie a piece of elastic to the sides of the mask to hold it on your head. Try to make different bird masks in the same way.

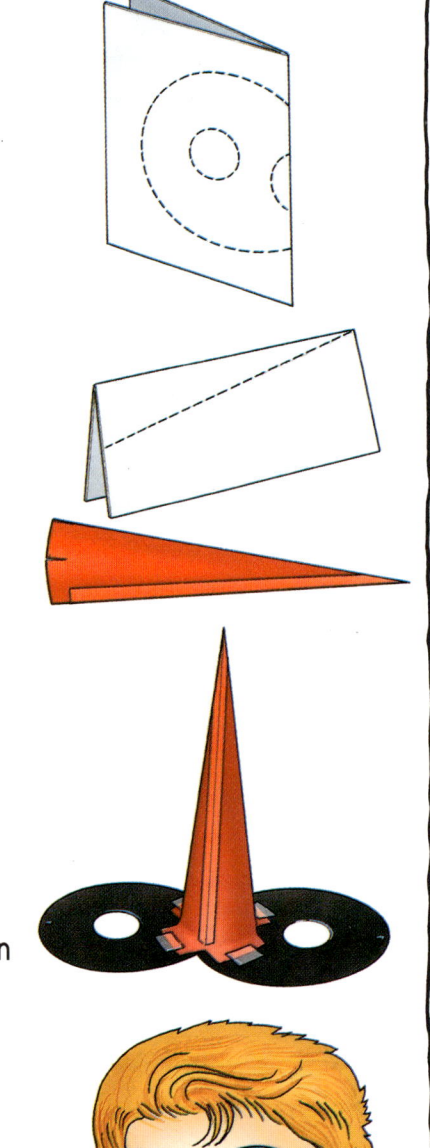

SHELL BOX

You can use shells you have collected to decorate things. Use a plain little cardboard box with a lid, or an empty matchbox. Stick shells all over it. When you have finished the box you can varnish the shells to make them shine.

BIRD MOBILE

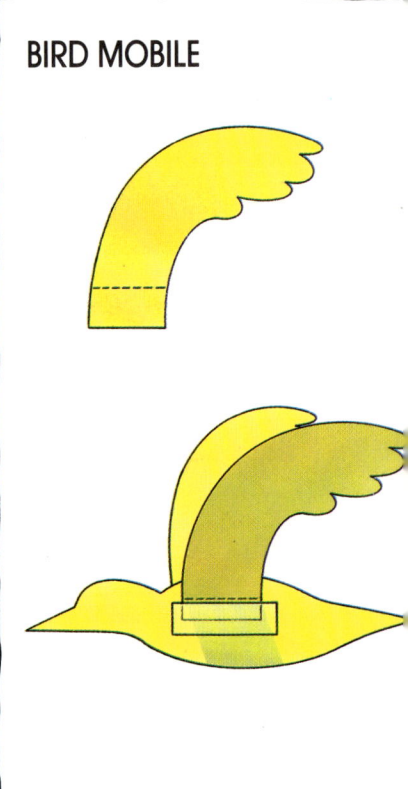

ROCK POOL COLLAGE

Try making a rock pool collage. Paint the rocks and the pool on paper. Use cloth or crepe paper to make seaweed and sea anemones. If you've got some shells use those or use shell pasta. Cut a starfish from a piece of sponge. Cut little fishes from silver foil. If you like, you could put cling-film over the picture to make it look as if it is under water.

SEA URCHIN SWEETS

You will need some marzipan and some flaked almonds to make these spiky sea urchin sweets. Roll small pieces of marzipan into balls. You can paint them with food colouring. Cut the flaked almonds into slivers – get an adult to help you with this. Stick the slivers into the marzipan ball to make the sea urchin's spines.

This is a way to make your own flying seabirds. You will need some thin card to draw the birds on. Don't draw the wings. Cut the birds out and colour them in. Fold a piece of paper and draw wings on it. Cut the wings out while the paper is still folded so you get two of each wing. Colour them in. Fold the end of the wings under and stick them to the birds' bodies with sticky tape.

When you have made the birds, tie them with thread to a piece of dowel. Tie thread to the dowel to hang your mobile up.

WORD LIST

buoy: a floating marker which shows sailors where dangerous things like rocks and sandbanks are under the water.

casts: little heaps of sand or mud shaped like a tube. This sand or mud has been through a worm's body. You can find worm casts lying on the wet beach when the tide is out.

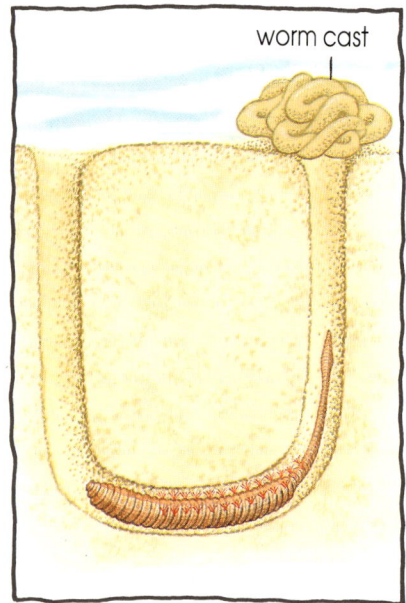

worm cast

harbour: an area of water by the seashore where ships can come close to the land in safety. The ships can also shelter from stormy weather in the harbour.

lifeboat: a special boat used to rescue people from the sea. The lifeboat is built so that it will roll upright if the sea tips it over.

lightship: a ship that is anchored near a sandbank or near some other danger under the sea. It has a bright light fixed to it to warn other ships to keep away.

naturalist: someone who studies plants and animals.

pier: a long platform built on legs out into the sea. Boats can tie up next to the pier. Sometimes there is an amusement arcade or theatre on the pier.

roost: to sit and sleep for the night. Birds roost.

sandbank: a high bank of sand under the water.

shellfish: sea animals that have shells to protect their soft bodies.

surfing: the sport of riding towards the shore on a board which is carried by a large wave.

waders: birds that get their food by paddling in shallow water. They poke their beaks into the sand or mud to find worms and other animals to eat. Some have very long beaks and long legs.

wet suit: a special suit which fits close to the body and keeps you warm when you are in water. It is often worn by divers.

wind surfing: this is a water sport. You balance on a board with a sail and the wind blows you along on the water.

INDEX

The **dark** numbers tell you where you will find information about the subject in a picture box.